How to keep your horse c

How to keep your horse calm and relaxed

TECHNIQUES FOR SCHOOLING AND COMPETING

Renate Ettl

The publishers recommend that all riders should wear correct clothing and a riding hat that meets current safety standards whenever they are riding or working with their horse. When riding on the roads it is important to be aware of local laws regarding horses on the road, to know the local highway code and to wear high-visibility clothing in order to be seen by other road users. If you are in any doubt about your horse's safety on the road, always ride with another rider until it is properly trained. Whilst every step has been taken to explain techniques carefully and in full, no responsibility can be accepted for any accident that may occur as a result of the instruction in this book.

Cadmos Verlag GmbH, Brunsbek
Copyright © 2006 by Cadmos Verlag
Typesetting and design: Ravenstein + Partner, Verden
Photos: Renate Ettl
Printers: Landesverlag, Linz
Edited by Jaki Bell
Translated by Ute Weyer

Printed in Austria
ISBN 978-3-86127-920-4

Content

The type of horse every-one wants to own.

The horse of your dreams

Nowadays, many people are able to fulfil their ambitions of owning a horse. However, that does not necessarily mean that your childhood fantasies of cantering a wild black stallion bareback across the hills, or riding the "Golden Mare" that wins one major championship after another will come true. Who does not wish to ride a fiery but obedient, elegant horse whilst the fans watch and applaud, even if it is only at a local competition?

The reality is often very different. Even if the dream of owning a horse is fulfilled, it can soon turn into a nightmare.

Your elegant steed may be a retired trotter, a lazy pony, a spooky Arab or a lethargic warm-blood. Of course it is prone to colic, has a splint, tendonitis or sweet itch, not to mention any abnormalities or back problems.

This would all be acceptable if, at least, the horse was pleasant to ride and did not explode at every possible opportunity. Even at small competitions, it loses its nerves and on a hack it storms off as soon as it hears a noise coming from a bush. Now riding is just stress instead of relaxation, and an easy hack has become a troublesome chore to exercise the horse.

This can only be corrected through long term and expert training so that communication between rider and horse improves and trust can develop. You may not be able to fulfil every dream, but by working towards realistic goals you can get fairly close to them.

One of the best ways to achieve your goal is to work with your horse in-hand with particular attention paid to confidence training as only calm horses are attentive and are able to learn. This is the basis for all other training.

A very relaxed equine athlete.

Understanding the horse's characteristics

Equine sport is relatively dangerous due to the fact that we are dealing with a living creature. It is, however, surprising that most accidents related to horses happen when handling a horse, not during riding. Kicking is at the top of the list of causes of injury, and biting follows close behind. One would think the biggest danger is falling off a horse but that is only the second most common accident.

Handling is more dangerous than riding

According to statistics from insurance companies, more accidents happen when handling horses than during actual riding. Therefore, a thorough training in this area is of utmost importance. In-hand work is a valuable tool to achieve this.

These statistics show that it is more dangerous to handle horses than to ride them. Why is this the case?

Accidents and the resulting injuries can be avoided by using safety equipment (helmet, gloves, boots and so on) and also with thorough training. A rider's ability can also be quite varied, depending on the riding school at which they were taught, and their ambitions, but many riding schools do not teach handling techniques at all.

It seems to be more important to show students how to jump a fence properly, yet how a rider should handle a horse is neglected. This, however, is important not only for the safety of the handler, but also to improve communication between horse and rider. Only when you know a horse's natural behaviour can you anticipate its reaction and act accordingly.

Natural behaviour of the horse

The horse's natural behaviour is as apparent when it is being handled as when it is ridden. The main features are the herd instinct and the flight reaction of the horse.

It is also essential to know how a horse perceives its environment in order to understand its reactions and to anticipate them.

Horses are flight and herd animals. If one gets frightened the whole herd will run away.

A horse has a completely different field of vision to a human. The position of the eyes allows the horse to have an almost completely circular view. However, there are blind spots in just a small area behind and in front of it. The areas either side, that are only visible with one eye, cannot be seen as three-dimensional, which makes judging distances difficult. In addition, a horse cannot focus very well, which may cause it to be afraid, but it can see objects from a long distance.

The senses of hearing and taste are much better developed than those of humans. A horse will react to stimuli that it can smell or hear of which a human will not be aware at all. In this case it is difficult for the rider to understand why his horse shows a certain reaction.

The flight animal

All animals can be roughly divided into two groups: predators and prey. Humans, cats and dogs belong to the first category. Horses, rabbits or antelopes belong to the latter. Predators have learnt to refine their hunting and attacking techniques. Prey animals, on the other hand, need to improve their ability to flee at any time in order to have a chance of survival.

For example, they need to be able to react very quickly when they recognise danger, and flee. The faster a horse can switch from peaceful grazing to flight, the harder it is for a predator to catch it. Horses have mastered this skill extremely well and this can present a problem for the rider.

A modern horse's living environment has changed completely, yet its instincts have stayed the same. Therefore, a sudden noise, smell or movement will trigger a flight reaction - the horse would rather be safe than sorry.

In the wild, if a horse first stopped to establish whether a harmless bird in a bush was the cause of a noise, it would not survive. Far too often it would have encountered a predator and would be killed.

The flight instinct explains why a horse runs off in a panic for even the slightest reason. It cannot understand that such a reaction can be dangerous in its contemporary (and unnatural) environment. A horse does not think about whether to flee or not, the reaction is purely instinctive.

This explains why horses are still easily frightened and always ready to run off. As this is a very basic instinct, it is not possible to eliminate it through breeding or training but, to a certain extent, it can be controlled by a thorough education.

Just run!

Being easily frightened and always ready to flee are basic instincts of horses that were important for their survival. It is impossible to eliminate these through breeding or training, but they can be controlled.

Safety in numbers

Another basic instinct of horses that can cause problems for owners is the herd instinct. Some horses cling to others and can only be separated from them with great difficulty. For the same reason, some refuse to leave the yard and others demolish their boxes when they have to be in the stable on their own. These reactions are very natural as the herd provides life-saving protection to an individual. The need to live in a social group is therefore very strong. It is extremely difficult for a horse to feel safe in an unnatural environment without companions. In-depth training based on understanding, patience and sensitivity is required here.

A person has to be able to offer their horse a 'herd substitute', which is certainly not easy, as the human can be seen as a potential predator. One has to have a thorough understanding of a horse's nature in order to gain its trust and subsequently make it feel safe.

The herd offers maximum protection for an individual.

Emergency situations

The horse's natural behaviour and instincts usually play a part when accidents occur. Every incident that a horse does not understand may cause fear and consequently flight. In these circumstances, the rider is no longer able to control the situation by convincing the horse that it is not dangerous or by stopping it running away (for example, by using a strong bit).

Almost all recreational riders exercise their horses outside. In fields and forests, dangerous situations can easily and frequently lead to accidents. If training and education are of a low standard, a simple hack can turn out to be a high-risk exercise.

The ghost in the corner

This famous 'ghost' can turn up everywhere and at any opportunity. It can be caused by a sudden noise, movement or smell that instantly triggers a flight reaction. However, if a horse has learnt to trust its rider, it may not run off immediately when encountering something new.

There are other situations, of course, when the horse gets frightened, for example a pheasant taking off in front of it or a rabbit crossing the path. After an initial fright, the horse will realise that there is no danger and it will calm down again.

If, however, a tarpaulin is blowing in the wind, the horse cannot judge the danger, and therefore its only logical reaction is flight. How the horse will react in any given situation depends on previous experiences, training and its character but in principle, all unknown encounters are a potential source of danger.

Noisy machines and traffic

Tractors and combine harvesters can frighten a horse as much as noisy lorries or motorbikes. Even cars are not always considered harmless. Monsters with engines do not play a part in a horse's natural environment. Fortunately, horses usually get used to vehicles from an early age as they grow up amongst them.

But even horses that are accustomed to them may flee if on occasion they feel threatened by something huge and bulky. This can happen if the machine invades a horse's personal tolerance zone and gets too close. Every animal has an individual tolerance zone within which it does not accept intrusive companions or unknown, potentially dangerous, objects. Either flight or avoidance is the consequence.

If a horse is trapped in a corner and flight is not possible, it will try and fight the danger as a last resort. Its hooves are its most effective weapon and a horse can kick to

the front as well as backwards – and many a dent in a car has come about that way.

A trapped horse can defend itself by biting as well. The attack is usually directed against a companion or a person that gets too close.

What a horse does not know ...

Initially, a horse will react with insecurity and fear to all unknown situations. Fear can quickly develop into panic and horses will try and run away.

As these reactions can be very dangerous, a good training programme is always aimed at minimising the horse's fear in order to be able to control the flight reactions better.

Young and inexperienced horses are far more likely to run away from unknown dangers. It is often helpful to have a more experienced companion nearby that can offer some reassurance for the youngster. As horses pick up behaviourisms from each other, they will learn to better judge situations and potential hazards.

Help your horse to become acclimatised to tractors by exposing it to them when it is still a foal.

15

This also explains why many horses react completely differently when facing a challenge on their own compared to when confronted with one as a group. The herd is braver; the leaders have the courage to examine the scary object closer, and soon the less brave ones follow. Before long, they will also check it out for themselves. If on their own, however, this latter group would probably just stand in a corner and not dare to go a step closer. This is a good example of group dynamics and shows the horse's herd instinct.

As species-specific behaviour is often a problem when handling and riding a horse, consistent training is necessary to at least control these basic instincts. Therefore, each horse should undergo "confidence training" during its basic education. Working on the ground (or working in-hand) can help with this.

Why work inhand?

Several schools of training exist wherein groundwork and games play a role, for example, Parelli Natural Horsemanship, Equine Ethology, and Western riding, and many leading trainers put great store in incorporating groundwork into a training pro-gramme on a regular basis. In most cases, these techniques are used to establish the relationship between horse and rider. However, working from the ground can also be used to help a horse over-come fears that may cause it to spook or take fright.

Better safety for human and horse
If more horse owners carried out such training, accidents with horses might be significantly reduced. Horse riding does not have to be a dangerous sport if one adheres to safety regulations and puts effort into the education of rider and horse.

Many owners only consider this work as a possibility when they are unable to ride their horse for whatever reason. In reality, how-ever, this form of training greatly minimises the risk of accidents because horse owners and horses will practise techniques that improve their mutual confidence and therefore increase – often unconsciously – their own safety.

Building confidence

Working in hand should be incorporated into the training programme of every horse according to its abilities.

In-hand work can increase safety for horse and rider.

Benefits of in-hand work

Working in hand offers a new challenge for horse and rider and benefits everyday work. The training is suited for hobby as well as competition horses as even competition horses can benefit from the occasional reminder of how they are meant to behave when in hand and some will enjoy the distraction of another form of training.

Benefits for the rider

Apart from the already mentioned safety aspect and the possibility of creating a more interesting work schedule, in-hand work offers an alternative form of training that doesn't involve riding and can be used in certain circumstances when a horse is unable to be ridden. However, do not underestimate the amount of concentration and effort that this type of work demands from the horse and do not use these games if your horse is unwell. If you are at all in doubt, check with your vet. In-hand work can be of benefit to the green rider or horse, however it is important to have an experienced handler alongside in these circumstances, as this is a subtle form of training and the slightest error in reaction can have an adverse effect.

17

Obedience games can involve the whole family.

For riders with a new horse or that are new to competition, in-hand work tests and improves the horse's calmness. This is a basic requirement for competition and prepares the combination for their first outings.

It also develops easier communication between horse and human, and this in turn is beneficial for work under the saddle. The result is an overall better harmony between rider and horse.

To summarise, in-hand work helps to establish a pecking order between handler and horse, to introduce communication, to build up confidence, to establish trust, to improve safety, and to add variety to a training programme.

Are all breeds suitable?

Many factors are responsible for whether a horse is relaxed and calm or easily frightened. Apart

For riders with a new horse or that are new to competition, in-hand work tests and improves the horse's calmness.

from previous experiences, management, age and training level, the inherited character plays a role. The genetic make-up determines type, character and temperament and can only be altered slightly even with the best training.

Breeding, therefore, plays an important part in the underlying constitution of a horse and forms character, type and temperament. Certain genetic characteristics are breed-specific as well. For example, Arabs are said to be more sensitive and highly-strung while

19

cobs are generally placid but also stubborn at times. Of course, there are exceptions to the rule but general trends can still be seen.

A calm horse may take to in-hand work without any reservations, whereas a very sensitive horse might need much for patience, training and education. In-hand work can therefore also give a handler an insight into the character of the horse they are handling if they do not know it well.

Introducing obedience games

Throughout the equine world there are various types of competition open to horse owners, handlers and riders that require a level of skill in in-hand work. In many countries, these classes are only open to children. However in Germany there is a type of competition known as the Obedience test that is open to children and adults and horses over three years of age.

The purpose of this test is to improve the confidence of horse and handler and this is done via a series of challenges. These challenges build on the fundamental skills of the handler, developing all those attributes of in-hand work previously mentioned, and are of benefit to all equestrians. The obedience games featured later in this book are therefore based on the challenges of this test.

However before beginning on the obedience games, it is important to understand the basic principles of confidence training.

Now that's a confident horse!

Confidence training

Equipment for ground schooling

Once a horse has learned that there is nothing to be afraid of if a tarpaulin blows in the wind as a lorry drives past it on the road, a trustful co-operation is guaranteed.

This training needs to be planned properly in order to avoid creating even more fear and losing the horse's trust.

Using the right equipment is essential to avoid accidents and also to ensure proper communication between horse and human. The location for the training is very important. Depending on the type of lessons a large school is essential.

Always stay within fenced-in areas so that the horse, should it be very frightened, cannot run out onto the road. Ideally use a sand school or indoor school but a well-fenced pasture or small paddock will do as well.

After patient training a horse can be totally acclimatised to scary objects such as a tarpaulin. The publishers would recommend protective head and footwear in these circumstances.

Head collar and lead ropes

Use a strong head collar and lead rope for confidence training. The head collar has to be fitted properly and should not press on the horse's nose so that a pull on the lead rope will not obstruct its breathing. A head collar with padded poll and nose straps is recommended.

The lead rope should be fitted with a strong clip. Thicker lead ropes, as used by Western riders, are easier and safer to hold than thin lead ropes. Elastic or stiff lead ropes should not be used.

The lead rope needs to be long enough to allow sufficient slack. Never wrap it around your hand! If the horse gets frightened, the rope could tighten and squash your fingers and hand. You cannot let go of the lead rope and there is the danger of being dragged along by a horse that tries to run away.

A horse should never be tied up for any confidence training. If it gets frightened, it could panic and pull on the rope, hurt itself or even sustain serious injuries. After such an experience, tying up may even become a problem.

> ### Never tie a lead rope around your hand!
>
> The rope should be held so that you can let go should the horse suddenly pull on it. If the lead rope, however, is tied around your hand, it will tighten and you cannot let it go any more. This can result in a fatal accident.

Young and boisterous horses should be led using a chain. The handler should wear appropriate clothing, including good gloves and firm shoes.

If you have a young and boisterous horse, you can use a chain attached to the rope and run it across the back of the horse's nose, fastened on each side of the head collar. This allows more control over the horse. The chain should not be so long that you have to hold it in your hand as it could cause you a nasty injury if the horse pulled away violently. Also be aware that the chain can inflict pain on the horse and therefore you must be very gentle when using it.

It is also possible to use a bridle instead of a head collar. If you would prefer not to have to hold the reins, you can remove them and use a small strap between the rings and connect it to a lead rope (also used for lungeing). Alternatively you can run the lead rope through the inside ring, under the horse's chin, through the outside ring, up and over the poll and back down to clip on to the inside ring (as is sometimes also done when lungeing).

23

You could also use so-called split reins as favoured by Western riders because these are longer and open. They are also safer for the holder because of their smooth leather finish.

Suitable clothing

When exercising your horse, hard wearing and comfortable clothing is not only practical but also safer. In particular sturdy, strong shoes with a steel toecap are recommended as they protect your toes, should the horse accidentally step on you.

Avoid very loose clothes as these can get caught up, also very tight clothes that may prevent you from moving freely.

No matter how hot it may be in the summer, do not wear shorts and a T-shirt with thin shoulder straps. It does not take much to scrape skin on your shoulders and knees.

In all cases, whether you lead or lunge a horse, gloves are a must. A rope can easily be pulled through your hands, which can lead to nasty burns if you do not wear gloves. It is also always recommended that you wear a riding hat that meets the current safety requirements and keep hair tied back out of the way.

Always be safe

A riding hat is an essential piece of safety equipment for a rider as are gloves and good shoes. All are equally important for the safe handling of horses. Do not become negligent with safety issues, even if nothing has ever happened to you. One day it might, and that could be once too often.

It is very easy to ignore these basic safety requirements when working on the ground with your horse, especially as you get to know it better. However accidents are usually caused by influences out of your control and it is better to be well prepared than sorry.

Safety clothing checklist

Wear the following when training in-hand with your horse:
- Firm, strong shoes, ideally with steel toecaps
- Long, comfortable trousers
- Clothes that are neither too loose nor too tight
- T-shirts covering the shoulders
- Gloves are a must!
- A riding hat is always recommended

Additional equipment

Bandages or boots are recommended for the horse, especially when working with ground poles. Even careful horses can knock their legs on the poles and hurt themselves. Boots or bandages will help protect the legs from such damage.

Bandaging is not easy and takes time, and bandages that are not put on properly can slide down if they are too loose, or restrict the blood supply if they are too tight, therefore boots are recommended.

Begin your training work using subtle commands (voice, leg pressure, pointing with fingers) and only use a whip as a last resort. If necessary, you can use a dressage whip of about 1.20 metres in length as an "extended arm". A whip should not be used to punish a horse, as you do not want to scare it. You want your horse to listen to what you are asking him to do and not to respect the whip more than you.

When all commands are given accompanied by a whip, a rider or leader of a horse can become dependant on it, especially if the horse has never been taught to react to very gentle aids. A whip (or spurs for ridden work) should only be used if the horse does not react to these.

A horse will soon understand that it is better to obey these subtle commands rather than the whip or other forceful measures.

Before long, obedience will become routine, which will make a whip superfluous.

Introducing scary obstacles

It is important how a horse is introduced to a new situation or a scary object for the first time. If the encounter is negative, the horse will remember this experience and be even more frightened the next time. This not only happens if a horse gets scared by something and jumps away or hurts itself, but also if the rider pulls the reins very hard in fright.

Excessive mental or physical pressure can also increase the fear of certain tasks, objects or situations.

For example, if a horse is uncertain when asked to walk across a tarpaulin and the rider puts too much pressure on with the whip, this will only make the horse more frightened. It will then resist this challenge completely and be less and less prepared to even try.

Horses react very differently to each situation and you should never expect immediate perfection, just a gradual improvement. Training methods will depend on the individual horse – on type, level of education and previous experience – and rely on the sensitivity of the trainer.

A stick can be helpful as an "extended arm".

The aim of training is improvement.

Always finish a session on a positive note. Do not expect perfection, as this would be too demanding for the horse and could eventually lead to a negative result.

Reactions of different types of horses

Native breeds or working horses are usually quite relaxed when facing new challenges and rarely lose their nerve. They give the impression of not being particularly bothered by outside influences.

More sensitive types are Thoroughbreds, trotters, Arabs and warmbloods. They can panic at even the slightest movement. However amongst these breeds you can find more placid individuals but generally they are more highly-strung than their native counterparts.

First of all, it is important to establish what type of horse you are dealing with as only then you can set up a correct confidence training plan and cope with tricky situations. Take for example a horse being confronted with a tarpaulin for the first time. The horse refuses to cross the sheet. Ask yourself why: is it frightened or simply too stubborn to face the challenge? The answer is important before the trainer can take any further actions.

It is usually easy to recognise whether a horse is scared or stubborn. Moving sideways, pulling away, wide-open eyes, shaking and snorting are always signs of genuine fear.

Obstinate horses, on the other hand, will not move forward and seem uninterested and absent-minded. Horses in a nearby field or passing traffic are all of more importance. Stubborn horses do not show any interest in the supposedly scary object.

It seems to be straightforward to divide horses into these two categories. However, it is not that easy! There are in-between types that are insecure, but also do not want to try to understand the situation.

And then there is the question of why a horse is frightened of the tarpaulin. Is it because of previous bad experiences or simply uncertainty? Does the trainer appear worried and is he or she passing this on to the horse? The latter is quite often the case and responsible for owners completely misjudging their animal's character. Try therefore, with the help of a

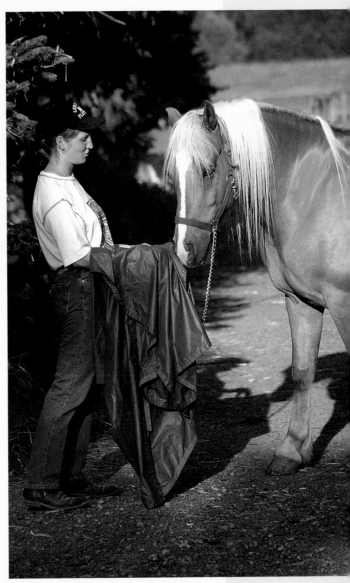

good trainer, to analyse your horse and the situation in question before beginning your training. Are you absolutely certain that your horse is genuinely frightened in a specific situation? Is it not just taking advantage? If it is frightened, you have to be patient and start confidence training carefully.

Introduce your horse to challenges sympathetically without force.

Know your horse

Before you are able to design a training schedule, you have to know why your horse reacts in a certain way. More often than not, a person passes his or her feelings on to their horse.

Getting your horse accustomed to bags

It is a good idea to begin with 'bag' training in order to gain your horse's trust. Start with an easy challenge and then increase the level of difficulty. Do not approach your horse with a huge tarpaulin to begin with, but with a small plastic bag (perhaps even containing a few treats like an apple or a carrot).

Use a head collar and lead rope, choose a quiet and safe location (not a busy stable yard with wheelbarrows and forks around) and take plenty of time!

When everything is to hand, you can start with the actual training. Approach your horse with a small bag. Show it what you are holding and let the horse examine the rustling bag with its nose. Slowly start running the bag over the horse's neck. If he does not show any resistance, include shoulders, back and legs. Only move on to each step when the horse has accepted the previous one.

If the horse shows fear, pulls away or raises its head, shakes or snorts, you have to stop for a while. By repeating this again and again, the animal will learn that there is nothing to be scared of and it will gradually lose its fear. Practise this for about 15 to 20 minutes every day and finish on a good note.

Start the next day with a task that the horse already knows or use an object that it has previously accepted and always praise it when it has accepted your challenge. Once he is happy with the bag you can move on to larger objects, such as a rug or even a piece of tarpaulin.

Don't forget:

Patience is the key to success, especially with frightened horses!

It is impossible to say how long it will take before a horse accepts a certain object. It differs from horse to horse and depends on many factors. Previous experiences are as important as the mental constitution. The everyday well-being plays a part as well, and do not be surprised if the horse works well one day and is frightened again the next. Be patient with your horse and never lose your temper! Only by being tolerant and calm will you achieve good

results. Harsh words or even punishment are completely counter-
productive because trust has to be
built and cannot be forced.

Sometimes the owner's patience
will be tested. There are situations
that a horse will never really
accept. It will always stay slightly
uncertain and the owner has to
learn to live with that. It is
important to recognise a horse's
psychological limits. You can
work up to these limits but
should not go beyond them, as
you will only fail to get results.
Identifying this fine line requires
a lot of understanding of a horse's
nature, experience and sensitivity.
Failure should not demoralise you,
often horses simply need a lot
time.

Stubborn horses

It is a totally different story when
a horse does not show any signs of
fear but simply refuses to do as
you ask. There can be many reasons for this. Apart from specific
characteristics including a strong
will and obstinacy, there is the
possibility that the horse does not
want to solve a particular problem. It might be that it does not
feel up to the challenge or simply
tries to avoid difficulties out of
lack of interest.

Whatever the underlying reasons for this behaviour, it is certain that the horse is testing its
boundaries. How far can I go?

*Let your horse examine the
tarpaulin first before trying
to run it over its body.*

What pressure will the owner
apply in order to get what he or
she wants? Is the handler stronger
than the horse? When does a handler give in? The horse is challenging a human's dominance.
Depending on how a person reacts
in this case, new rankings will be
established.

If you proceed too quickly you will frighten your horse

If you are absolutely sure that your horse is not frightened, it is then important to enforce what you ask of it. Especially intelligent horses know precisely what they can achieve by being stubborn. Often the rider gives up and takes the horse back to the stable, which is exactly what the horse wanted.

Who is the boss?

If you ask a horse to do something then you have to insist that it is carried out. If you are not sure whether your horse is able to do it, it is better not to try it at all, rather than lose your dominant ranking!

If you own a very confident horse you have no choice but to always enforce what you want from it. Every inconsistency can lead to losing your higher ranking. Therefore, be firm and overcome your horse's obstinacy with patience and consistency.

Humans as herd leaders

Whether your horse is frightened or stubborn – it is always important that Man is the leader. A timid horse will not be able to build trust and a confident horse will get the better of you.

As soon as a scared horse realises that the trainer is worried or nervous, it will be reluctant to follow and resist any task vehemently. Therefore, a determined, consistent and firm behaviour is very important.

Timid horses prefer a partner that will protect them. This can be another horse or a person, as long as they can be trusted. Being a herd animal, it will follow this companion everywhere and feel safe. In the wild, it is usually the alpha mare that will lead the herd. All others follow her and feel secure under her care. The leading mare makes sure that the herd grazes in safe locations and she will lead them on if the grazing area needs to be changed. If she disappoints her companions by choosing unsafe or poor grazing grounds, she will soon lose their trust and therefore her leading position.

Even stubborn or very confident horses accept that the alpha mare will set the boundaries and earn respect. It is often only necessary for her to put her ears back in order to admonish a herd member that is misbehaving, although sometimes she has to use stronger methods. On occasion, she has to resort to a kick or bite to remind the others who is the boss.

... the horse then tries to run away.

Human beings need to imitate the behaviour of the leading mare if they want to keep the alpha position. For safety reasons alone, it is important that a person has a higher rank than the horse. Thus you teach a stubborn horse discipline and inspire a timid one to trust you.

Who is the boss?

Some horses have trained their owners really well. They decide when they have worked enough or who goes through the stable door first. This animal will snatch a mouthful of feed before the person has a chance to tip it into the trough and a foot is only held up for as long as this four-legged friend fancies. The owner often does not even notice how much their horses have taken control. It may be that both of them – horse and rider – are quite happy with this situation, but the owner has usually misjudged the horse's behaviour completely.

If a horse does not want to work any more in the school, the rider often interprets this as exhaustion. You have to ask yourself though: "Is my horse exhausted or simply not willing to work any more?" More often than not the animal has lost interest and become stubborn.

In situations like this, the rider has to insist if he does not want to lose his alpha position. He should,

however, ask himself why the horse does not want to work any more. Is the workload too boring or too repetitive? Is it too difficult or too easy? A horse will enjoy an interesting, challenging (but not over-demanding) training programme and such a situation can be avoided.

Between wanting and being able to

If a horse refuses to carry out certain work, the trainer has to establish whether it just does not want to do it, or whether it is actually not capable of doing it. Only then can they react correctly.

Make sure, especially with very confident horses, that you are the boss! Otherwise you are at the horse's mercy.

Problem cases

As mentioned before, it is not always possible to classify your horse as stubborn or frightened and a straightforward division like this can only be a rough guideline. A horse's reaction to a certain situation is not only determined by its character but depends on many factors.

This means that simple classification is not always possible. Consider this before you start on your training programme, especially if you have a difficult horse, in order to avoid making mistakes that you will regret later. Always try to identify the reasons for your horse's behaviour but do not be judgemental. Every incorrect judgement may lead to further erratic behaviour and therefore failure of your training purpose. If in doubt, ask an experienced trainer for help.

Mistakes in management

A horse's physical and mental wellbeing depends on how it is kept and fed. The physical condition has a great influence on behaviour. Horses can also have a bad mood, and then tend to react negatively. This bad mood can be caused by hunger or by seeing other horses having fun in the field while it is forced to work.

There are many reasons for every type of mood. Weather influences and the daily rhythm can play a part as well. Horses are often very frisky when it is windy and tend to shy more often, for example, and hot and humid weather can lead to horse and rider feeling listless and tired.

Daily differences

Humans are not the only ones to suffer from changes in the weather, horses can be affected, too. Feeling depressed when it is grey and cold, or tired when very humid, can be typical symptoms for both. Weather can influence the daily mood of all living beings.

Separation from companions, insufficient exercise, dark stables and lack of stimulation are the root of many equine psychological problems and increase fear and nervousness significantly. Species-specific stable management can prevent many behavioural problems right from the beginning. It is ideal to keep horses in a herd

Correct feeding is an important factor of a horse's wellbeing and balance.

Horses that are exposed to many environmental stimuli on a daily basis are usually less timid.

with access to open stables but you have to pay attention to selecting a suitable group. Otherwise life in the herd can create a lot of stress, especially when turn out area is limited. Even just two horses together constitute a small herd. Experience has shown that small herds – and preferably of even numbers – are ideal.

Correct feeding is part of species-specific management. Very often pleasure horses are overfed. They are given too much energy in their feed, which is then not used up in their daily exercise. Highly bred horses and ponies that are fed a lot of concentrated food, despite doing very little work, are particularly sensitive and can display erratic behaviour like running away or extreme fear. Feeding must meet the actual demand of energy. Horses only need hard feed if they are worked regularly. The pleasure horse that is only hacked out occasionally will do fine on just maintenance food. High quality fodder and some mineral supplement form the basis. Hard feed like oats, barley or commercial mixes only need to be added with increased workload.

Suitable feeding and stable management assure a horse's physical and mental wellbeing. These are the best ingredients for successful training.

Bad experiences

If a horse does not get used to objects and situations like the tarpaulin, rustling bag or traffic, bad previous experiences can be the cause for this. Horses have a very

If a horse has had a bad experience with a particular obstacle, it will be difficult to correct this.

good memory and they will not forget negative experiences. A horse that had an accident whilst travelling in a trailer will often refuse to ever go into one again. Traumatic events can occur without the owner realising or recognising them. Many horse owners cannot therefore understand why their horses are so frightened of a particular object and it is not easy to discover the cause. It is important though, to be even more patient in order to work through such a trauma. A horse may never completely lose its fear and you should be satisfied if you can achieve at least some improvements.

Bad experiences can mean many things: a horse may simply feel that it cannot cope with a certain situation, and that can be an indication of too demanding training; or an injury received that has caused it to now connect the pain with this particular incident or object.

After a bad experience you will have to start to correct the situation and it can take three times longer than teaching an inexperienced horse the same thing. Most traumas cannot be completely overcome. A horse in this position will remain a bit suspicious, which of course is very understandable.

First steps over ground poles

Working with obstacles

Before working with obstacles, make sure that they are accident proof. For example, a horse can get trapped in a hole in a tarpaulin and panic. This can completely ruin a careful training programme, as well as presenting a significant risk of injury for the horse. The same goes for 'bridges'

that are slippery or weak. Protruding nails or wood splinters are also very dangerous and fences should be checked carefully before being used for training.

You may encounter hazardous fences even at small competitions. Think about your horse's welfare and do not blindly trust the organisers. Avoid suspicious looking jumps and, if necessary, withdraw.

Unsuitable fences are, for example, very steep 'bridges' that can lead to the horse slipping, or ropes (used as boundary lines or similar) or car tyres, in which the horse can trap its feet.

Obstacles that are too difficult for your horse should also be avoided. If your horse has never stepped over poles before, you should not raise them or arrange them in complicated grids. Successful training always depends on how you introduce new fences. Never ask your horse to fulfil a challenge if you are not sure whether it is physically and mentally able to do so, and ensure you make your horse carry it out properly.

Stepping over fences

There are several categories of obstacles that require different solutions and also specific preparation. There are the so-called confidence building obstacles, including the rattling bag, tarpaulin, or bridge. Poles and bridges are fences horses need to step over, and most horses find that easy or only a small problem. Confidence is less of a problem than experience in doing these. The more the horse pays attention to where to place its feet, the better it can cross the obstacle.

Using poles

The possibilities of how to use poles are almost endless and the level of difficulty varies signifi-

cantly as well. It can just be a single pole on the ground that the horse needs to step over, or several raised and crossed arrangements. Always start with a simple design before introducing anything complicated.

As a starter, an arrangement of two, later building up to five poles at an equal distance to each other is recommended. If you walk over them, the distance between each should be between 40 to 70 centimetres depending on the size and pace of your horse. Later on, trainer and horse should be able to walk through a wider or narrower and more uncomfortable distance equally well. The horse then has to adjust its length in stride according to the distance between the poles.

Judging distances

At first, the novice horse should encounter comfortable distances between the poles so that it can fulfil this task with satisfaction. The ideal distance is different for every horse as it depends on the length of stride. In walk, it is about 40 to 70 centimetres, in trot 50 to 120 centimetres and in canter 180 to 250 centimetres.

The aim of using the poles is that the horse steps over them without touching them with its feet. It should carry out this task carefully and attentively. You should allow your horse to inspect the obstacle thoroughly beforehand. Only ask it to walk across the poles once it is fully aware of them and lowers its head to inspect them.

Walk confidently ahead of your horse when leading your horse over the poles so that it actively lifts its legs. Very often poles are not taken seriously enough and

the horse touches them with his feet, which can lead to injuries. A clumsy horse might even stumble and possibly damage the coronet band.

If necessary you can use your stick and lightly touch the horse's feet if it is too lazy and does not want to lift its leg. Encourage it to be more active and never forget to reward it when it has carried out an exercise well. If your horse does not pay attention or touches the poles respond with a loud "pay attention" or "no".

A horse has to step over poles actively without touching the wood. This youngster takes the task very seriously.

Working the horse through this arrangement of poles backwards is an interesting and challenging exercise.

If this does not help, you can pull the reins firmly a few times to make it pay attention.

It is useful to move quickly on to create more complex designs with the poles in order to avoid boredom. You can lay them out in a W- or Z-shape, raise one or two, build a square, an L or U. You can then cross these different shapes from all sides. Generally, you should lead your horse in a straight line and across the middle of an obstacle so that it cannot easily avoid it and is better co-ordinated. If your horse is more advanced, you can deliberately make it cross the poles at an angle, which will increase its co-ordination and concentration further.

An interesting exercise is to work your horse backwards across one and then two poles and this can be increased to an L-shape (see photo left) or even a maze.

If you are ambitious, you can even ask your horses to cross the poles sideways. There are no limits, but always make sure that you do not push your horse too far. Gradually increase the challenge.

The bridge

Bridges and seesaws are not common in the UK. A bridge forms part of western trail classes, but the seesaw is rare and tends to be confined to riding demonstrations. If you are not competing in western classes, only include these in your training if you are a very experienced horse handler. The same rules apply as for the poles: first lead your horse towards the bridge in a straight line and in the middle. Let it explore the obstacle and only then ask it to step on it.

You can also let your horse cross the poles sideways – from the ground, as well as under the saddle.

41

Seesaws are very unusual in the UK. Chances are you would have to have one made specially for you if you wanted to include it in your training.

Some horses are scared of the hollow sound their feet make when stepping on the wood.

Some bridges have banisters and are quite small; this might make certain horse hesitate or even refuse to step on them. Patience is the only way forward. If possible, practise with bridges without banisters and let your horse cross them sideways. This is only possible with bridges that are straight and not too high. Many Western riders favour so-called round

bridges and these should not be crossed sideways.

The wooden surface of the bridge can be slippery when wet, which is dangerous. A bit of sand or sawdust spread on it will help. It is better, though, to cover the bridge when it is raining or store it indoors somewhere.

Seesaws are no longer popular as several accidents have occurred as a result of training with a seesaw. It is also an artificial obstacle as moving surfaces should always be avoided for safety reasons when out on a hack.

Most horses, however, will cross a seesaw as easily as a bridge. If you really think your horse will benefit from this training, you will probably have to have a seesaw made for you. It is, of course, important to make sure that the boards are strong enough and will not break. Also make sure that the seesaw is long enough. A horse has to stand on it with all four legs before the seesaw tilts forward – at least 2.5 meters. If the seesaw tilts forward while the hindlegs are still on the ground, severe injuries can happen.

Be prepared for an inexperienced horse to be frightened and possibly to jump off the seesaw when it starts to move. Most horses learn quickly what this obstacle does and some horses actually enjoy the movement and do not want to get off.

Everything that rustles

Horses are suspicious of objects that produce a rustling or hissing sound. Sensitive and nervous horses, in particular, have to be introduced to rustling objects very slowly and with lots of patience. Getting used to this challenge belongs to the category of confidence tests.

In our modern, technical world, horses are confronted with unusual situations more and more often. Therefore, confidence training should be incorporated into every training schedule in order to prepare horses, especially nervous ones, to cope better with numerous unexpected hazards. Animals that have encountered many different situations and objects are more confident and have greater trust in humans. All these factors make a horse a safer companion and many accidents can be avoided. Training with flapping and rustling objects is very important.

Bags, tarpaulin and tape

Facing a bag or a big plastic cover, carelessly thrown away, whilst out on a hack, can be a horrifying experience for a horse. Often, the very bright or extremely dark colours of agricultural tarpaulins are frightening enough, but usually the fast movements of a flapping plastic sheet are the scariest. The sounds the plastic covers make are not something a horse enjoys. It is no surprise that a horse will shy away from these and would rather run off.

The frightening properties of a bag or a tarpaulin can soon lead to a dangerous situation. Therefore, the animal has to be introduced to these with patience and persistence. Horses that start to panic when seeing a flapping object are frightened. They should never be punished for their fear and it

time, instead of overcoming its fear. In most instances, a horse jumps a little when scared and then calms down again. It is therefore worth trying to hold the reins loosely and use your voice to soothe it. A firmer use of reins is only justified, in order to prevent a dangerous situation, if the horse is so frightened that it tries to flee in panic.

Fear must not be punished

Horses that are scared or shy with fear should never be punished for it. Punishment will only increase their fright. You can only reduce fear with calm and patient handling.

Naturally, humans react instinctively too and often automatically pull the reins when frightened themselves. You can, however, learn to stay calm and to react sensibly.

With increasing experience and effort, this will eventually become second nature.

If a person sets an example and is relaxed around tapes, bags and tarpaulins he shows the horse that these are not dangerous objects. Horses learn from their companions – and also from humans. If you handle a tarpaulin with too much caution (because you believe your horse might take fright) the

This pony is familiar with the clatter bag used at home. But would it react differently in a strange place with an unusual bag?

would only increase their fright if you pull the reins hard or even punish it with your whip. A horse will connect a frightening object, such as a tarpaulin, with the pain and run away even sooner next animal will connect a certain danger with the object.

On the other hand, you must not push your horse to the limits by making loud rustling noises and rushing around with a tarpaulin. If your horse shies away, then it is showing you that it cannot cope with the situation. Only confront it with as much as it is able to accept.

Start your training with small bags and increase their size up to a large sheet. Also increase the noise level by rustling the plastic. Use tarpaulins of different materials and colours. A white one is not the same as a black one. For the horse, lorry covers are different to red and white plastic tape. Change objects and noise levels and also locations. Only then can your horse learn to relax in unexpected situations.

Dragging objects behind

In the wild, predators attack horses from behind and bite their flanks. That is the reason why equines are afraid of something approaching them from behind. Their blurred vision also contributes to them being jumpy. Delaying flight until they have identified what is going on behind them could be too late. A horse will therefore run away instead of analysing a situation first.

In Germany, a popular, hand-made object to help horses become accustomed to something coming along behind is a 'clatter bag'. It is a strong hessian or plastic bag filled with empty cans. The cans clatter significantly and many horses are frightened of the noise. The difficulty is not only the suspicious noise but also the fact that the noise is coming from behind. When dragging a clatter bag behind a horse, it can sometimes try to escape. This is not necessarily because it is frightened of the actual object but more because it cannot see it properly. For example, a simple branch could replace the clatter bag and the horse may still be scared.

If your horse is sensitive to noise, you could begin by practising dragging other objects, such as poles, rugs or tarpaulins. This is a particularly valuable exercise for horses that are to be used for driving.

You can practise from the ground or under saddle. Firstly, ensure the horse accepts the rope that will pull the object, as some horses will kick as soon as a rope touches their rump or legs. If the horse does not accept this contact, you need to resolve that problem first.

Other ideas

If you use your imagination, there are no limits to the new situations you can design that can

Place objects in the paddock for the horse to become accustomed to. Curiosity usually overcomes fear, but make sure that the horse cannot hurt itself.

build confidence. As long as you do not ask too much from your horse, it will enjoy getting to know new objects and circumstances. Some horses will be very keen on playing with things (and dismantling them). This fights boredom and the horse will find learning fun.

In order to familiarize a horse with a new object that it is unsure or even scared of, you could place the object in its paddock; but of course only if it is not a hazardous item that could lead to injuries when the horse plays with it. For example, large plastic sheets are excluded, as the horse could become entangled in them, whereas large balls are safe to use.

If a horse is kept in the stable and is easily frightened you should not confront it with these objects. Do not back it into a corner. Your four-legged friend should always have enough space to retreat to safe ground. Therefore, a stall is not ideal, but you could use a sufficiently large turn out area.

Horses will usually approach the scary object after a while because they are curious and get easily bored. This does not always work as sometimes the fear remains stronger than the curiosity, but it is certainly worth a try.

46

Balls and balloons

Plastic balls in all sizes are excellent items for training as they are not dangerous. Horses are fascinated by the fact that balls bounce off the ground or walls and they may suspect them to be unpredictable. The size of the ball is important, too, and you should start with a small ball to get the horse familiar with them.

It's a good idea to begin with a massage ball and rub your horse with it all over its body, according to the instructions. Normally, horses are not afraid of such a small ball. Deliberately drop the ball and observe your horse's reaction.

If the horse remains calm, use a bigger ball and also rub it over the whole body. Let that drop on the floor as well. If the horse stays relaxed, you can start to bounce the ball along the ground, pass it to another person over the horse's back or roll it underneath its belly. You can also roll a soft ball against the horse's legs as long as it accepted the previous procedures calmly and patiently.

Eventually you will want to introduce a physiotherapy ball. This ball is often initially scary for the horse because it is so big. Once they have got used to it, however, you can start playing a round of horse-football, which is great fun.

Balloons, whilst possible, have to be used with caution. Although

Balls of all sizes can be excellent training objects.

horses get used to them quite quickly, they can suddenly burst, frightening the horse - and you will have to start your confidence training all over again. Eventually, horses should become accustomed

47

to bursting balloons. Keep the balloon at a safe distance and let it pop. Check your horse's reaction. If it's okay, you can begin to reduce the distance. Some horses even step on balloons themselves to make them burst!

Brooms, bins and trailers ...

However, there are sufficient scary objects in the horse's environment. Even close to the stable frightening objects, such as tractors, suddenly appear and can cause some horses to shy. Whilst a few horses will never get used to these huge vehicles, if you take your time and introduce them carefully, most horses will lose their fear in the end. A farmer can then drive past your horse at full throttle without causing any reaction, which is the aim of this particular type of confidence training. When practising with vehicles, never let a tractor or motorbike drive straight towards the horse because it may see this as an attack and become scared. It is better to lead the horse towards the vehicle so that it can realise that this is not dangerous. You can then ask someone to drive past the horse. This should be done at various speeds, depending on the tolerance of your horse, in order to expose it to the various sounds and sights.

Brooms can be frightening objects, in some cases, because there are horse owners that use them to chase their horses, for example, into a trailer. Try and brush your horse with a (soft) broom. Is it scared? In that case, you have something to practise with.

There are many things that a horse can be frightened of. Bins, feedbags or car tyres – these are all objects that a horse does not necessarily take for granted. You can never predict what might or might not be scary. Some do not even mind a combine harvester that suddenly appears from behind, while others panic at the noise of a small bird in a bush.

Different circumstances

Sometimes horses will surprise you. A horse that was scared of plastic tape will suddenly walk through a curtain made of the same flapping fencing tape without blinking an eyelid. The reason is that it is not the tape alone that causes the fright but the entire situation. Does it flap in the wind? Is it vertical or horizontal and at what height? Are there many ribbons or just one? How is the horse confronted by it? All these factors play a part.

Brooms can be frightening. Some horse owners use them to encourage their horse into the trailer.

A good confidence exercise is to brush the horse with a broom.

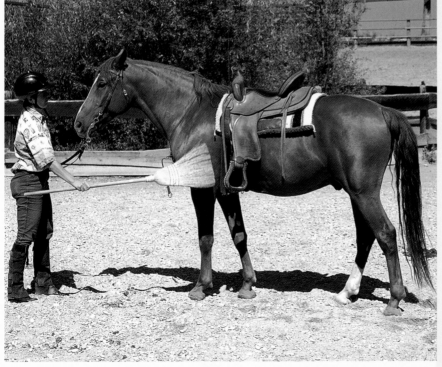

A bad experience in a trailer often causes fear. Trying to load in a hurry, or driving carelessly, can both lead to the horse connecting the trailer with a negative event. It is therefore no surprise when the horse subsequently refuses to load again. It is important to stay calm yourself, if you want your horse to remain cool.

Smells and sounds

It does not have to be an object that causes a horse to be frightened. Horses have very good hearing and their sense of smell is far better than that of humans. It was vital for horses in the wild to be able to recognise a predator quickly through sound and smell and so horses are very sensitive in these respects.

Many horses find the smell and grunting of pigs quite spooky. A flock of sheep can cause it to run away if it has never seen, smelt or heard them before. Horses cannot interpret the sounds of other animals: are these warning calls or forms of greeting? How can a horse understand another species' language, if it has not encountered these animals before?

Hissing and whistling sounds are especially fearsome. Most horses dread the sound of a spray bottle. Maybe it hurts their ears? And hissing sounds are often warning signals - think of snakes, for example.

It is possible to get horses accustomed to these hissing noises by exposing them to the sound frequently and connecting the sound to a reward.

The same obstacle – a new danger?

Most riders have encountered the situation when training has been going very well at home, but at a competition your horse is scared of every fence as if it had never seen one before. This is not rare and many horse owners are at a loss in these circumstances.

It is difficult to understand that a horse accepts an object without problems one day and is scared of it the next. As this appears illogical to people, it is often misinterpreted. You may think that the horse just does not want to perform and is just being stubborn, as it knows the fence and was not scared of it yesterday. When this happens, many a horse owner unfortunately uses the whip or punishes his horse with harsh words.

If you truly understand a horse's nature, however, you will not be surprised by these reactions. Horses think differently to humans and, of course, show different behaviour. The same obstacle can present a totally new challenge from one day to the next.

For example, it can appear completely changed at a different time of day or in different light.

When the right side doesn't know what the left side's doing

A fence appears completely new to a horse when led towards it from a different side. A riding exercise, for example a small circle, flying change or half pass, is a very new lesson for a horse when carried out on a different rein.

Once a horse has learned a lesson on one rein, it will have to learn it again on the other. Horses cannot think in mirror image and reverse a task. A tarpaulin that it has learned to cross from one direction, is a totally new challenge when approached from the other side and a horse may suddenly refuse.

Unlike in humans, horse's left and right sides of the brain are not connected, which explains why obstacles present a new challenge when approached from a different side.

Frequent changes

As if it were not enough that a fence appears different from each side, even the smallest change is recognised as a completely new situation. If a ball is not red any more but green, if an umbrella is a bit larger, or if a pole has been moved to another place, a horse will view these as new obstacles.

An obstacle that seems impossibly scary from one direction can be easy from the opposite side.

51

Horses are very good observers and notice the slightest alterations.

It is therefore not surprising that a horse is uncertain when facing an apparently similar object at a competition, although it could pass it without problems at home. This is a characteristic that you can use in your training to build up your horse's confidence. You do not need to have a limitless supply of tarpaulins, barrels, balls and poles at your disposal. By repositioning an obstacle, you arrive at a fresh challenge to your horse and therefore, with very limited props at your disposal, you can invent a variety of different tasks.

Every part of your training increases your horse's general confidence but do not be disappointed if a horse suddenly becomes frightened by an umbrella despite having practised with umbrellas a lot at home. As explained, it's not only the obstacle, but also the whole environment and ambience, that has an essential influence on the horse's reactions.

Simple objects become the props for obedience games

Obedience games

Working on in-hand 'games' with your horse will help build your confidence handling your horse, as they establish that you have it under control and are able to lead it correctly. They will also help your horse to develop confidence in you, as he learns and understand what you are asking of him. The obedience games in this book are based on a German equestrian test. Unfortunately there is nothing similar in the UK. However the principles are applicable to all horses and horse owners and they can help to desensitise your horse to some of the situations and events that it may encounter whilst out riding.

Teach your horse to stand when you ask him to

Why play games?

There are four very good reasons for playing obedience games with your horse:

- they build up confidence for both you and your horse;
- they teach your horse to accept that you are in control;
- they help to desensitise your horse to some of the potential obstacles it might meet whilst out on a ride;
- they help you to prepare for many of the competition classes that include in-hand work.

Begin by teaching your horse to stand at halt on command. Lead it to a pre-determined spot and make sure it stands square. If necessary, ask it to move back by gently applying pressure on the chest until it stands square.

Practise this at home and insist that your horse stands patiently until you ask it to move again. You should be able to do this with your horse in a head collar and lead rope, but as most in-hand classes take place with the horse in a bridle, practise in your bridle too.

Trotting in hand

For the purpose of our obedience games, the horse is led from the left or near side. This was the traditional side from which to lead, however it is now acknowledged that it is important to be able to lead your horse safely from both sides.

Why do I need to trot up my horse?

You may need to trot your horse up for the vet or the farrier to see whether he is sound. This is not the time to discover that your horse will not trot up in a straight line!

Here's an example of how not to lead a horse, whether for games or otherwise.

Turn a half circle to the right and begin your trot as soon as you are level with the cone.

Keep the trot active and your horse is more likely to go straight.

between them. Leading your horse to the right, come around the bottom cone and, as you straighten up and come level with the cone, start to trot. Head towards the next marker in a straight line. When you reach the marker, return to walk immediately and lead your horse around the marker to the right, once more. As soon as he is straight, and level with the cone, start trotting again. When you arrive back at your starting point, return to walk. Your aim is for your horse to break into trot at the point of the cone or marker. He should trot exactly next to you, with your shoulder level with his shoulder and he should try neither to run away, nor be allowed to fall behind. In the first stages you may need to say 'trot' or click your tongue but your horse should soon recognise your body movements and do this exercise without verbal signals from you.

Tips for a better trot

Your horse should display an even, active trot. You may need to stretch out your arm a little bit in order not to pull his head to the left or right. Even at walk, lead your horse at a good pace so that the transition to trot is made easier. You will also animate your horse to use his hind legs more, which is good exercise for him.

Set two cones or markers in a straight line as shown in the photographs with at least 4 metres

An active trot will help to improve rhythm and momentum. If you trot too slowly many horses will not be straight and may drag their feet. This does not look pleasant and does them no good. You may also need to practise the downward transition from trot to walk. If this presents a problem, until you have this mastered, do not try to do too active a trot, as you may lose control of your horse. These downward transitions will require practice.

Surprises in hedges

If your horse naps at the slightest sound in a hedge, this game is for him. Your aim is to walk your horse in a straight line past a wall or hedge that can be real or especially constructed for the game. At some point a bunch of balloons should suddenly appear from behind the wall. Your horse must continue on the set path, without swinging or jumping to left or right or trying to run away.

Well prepared! This horse remains calm when the balloons suddenly appear from behind the wall.

Keep the wall, which can be made up of fence poles and tarpaulins or rugs, to your left and get a helper to hide behind it with the balloons.

What can go wrong?

Very few of us will actually have a convenient wall or hedge to use for this exercise and will have to resort to improvising with wings, poles, rugs and tarpaulins. For this reason, it is important that you accustom your horse to the sight of rugs and tarpaulins hanging over poles. Be prepared for the inexperienced horse to try and run off initially.

To practise, use whatever you have available to build a fence in your school and place a familiar rug over it. Ask a helper to stay hidden and flap the rug while you lead your horse past. If your horse accepts this action, increase the challenge by using a rain cover, and then moving on to a large tarpaulin.

Your horse should not only accept this situation, but eventually even become bored with it. When that happens, it's time to go on the next step. Before the balloons appear from behind the wall, practise with a few simpler objects, such as buckets, branches or even flags, first. The aim is that the horse does not get scared when unexpected objects emerge. Make sure you frequently change the appearance of the fence and the point at which the object is going to appear, in order to avoid the horse becoming complacent. Once your horse is happy with visual surprises, try gradually introducing sounds behind the wall such as electrical equipment, music or sudden bangs. Remember to progress slowly and gradually and give your horse plenty of time to become accustomed to these new sights and sounds. Your aim is to acclimatise him to them, not to scare him.

Finally introduce the balloons. Once he is happy with their strange appearance, you could try bursting them as well. However, do not attempt this near to the horse's head. Even if he is perfectly calm, it may hurt his ears.

After practising this game thoroughly, your horse should remain completely cool when hacking past any challenges in or behind a hedge!

Fair – secure – relaxed

Always lead your horse confidently past these obstacles. By paying no attention to potentially dangerous objects you will give your horse enough confidence to remain calm. It is an effective and secure method for practising and demonstrating coolness.

Cross poles

Every well-trained horse should be familiar with poles on the ground. Even a horse too young to be ridden should be introduced to such obstacles, so that it is already familiar with them when it is worked under the saddle.

For this game, the poles need to be arranged in a square, measuring about 1.70 metres on the inside, and they have to be placed on top of each other (see photograph) at the corners, to prevent them from rolling away. Arrange them so that one end lies underneath the adjacent pole and the other end lies on top of its neighbour. Make sure that the crossing points are clear enough for your horse's feet (see photograph).

The challenge is to lead the horse diagonally across the square. It has to step over the poles at the crossing points. It must not step over them sideways or touch or move the poles.

The aim of this task is to teach the horse to cross an obstacle on the ground without being a risk to rider or leader, and without hurting itself. A certain amount of responsibility and independence is necessary on the part of the horse, but he must not take complete control.

This task looks relatively easy but has some hidden difficulties. Only rarely are horses frightened of the poles, but they find it hard to step into the square properly and some tend to step onto their owners' feet or push them away, so be careful.

The person leading the horse has to walk their horse to the crossed poles confidently. The horse should pay attention as is demonstrated here perfectly.

59

Frequent mistakes and how to avoid them

A horse that tries to pull to one side may have problems with its co-ordination and therefore wants to avoid the poles. In the wild, a horse will always stay away from an obstacle, if at all possible. Our domesticated pleasure and competition horses, however, have to learn to carry out these tasks. Normally, horses can be convinced quite easily to step over the poles.

Before you attempt to lead your horse across the poles you have to make sure that it has taken a proper look at where it is going. Let it examine them first, so that it can evaluate the difficulty, and only then continue.

If a horse cannot see the poles clearly, it will most likely touch them with its feet. It may even stumble or jump away and in a worst-case scenario injure itself. This can happen if you do not allow it to lower its head and look at the obstacle properly. Let the rein go and encourage your horse to have a good look and only then ask it to step across.

In the beginning, walk the animal towards the poles in a straight line so that it will notice them early enough, but move on to leading the horse across the square from all angles in order to improve its co-ordination and balance.

If your horse is lazy and drags its feet across the poles, you can use a whip or your voice to encourage it to be more active. Do not accept that it touches the poles, but react with a sharp "no" or "pay attention" or alternatively pull the lead rope briefly to wake it up.

If your horse is accustomed to using the poles on the ground in its schooling, you may have a problem leading it across them in walk. It may want to jump the corners or, if energetic, may even try and jump across the whole square.

In these circumstances, you have to teach your horse very slowly that a 10 centimetre high pole does not have to be jumped, but that it is okay to simply walk over it. Sometimes, cavalletti training carried out in trot can be helpful. This provides a new challenge and also increases fitness and strength.

Walk your horse towards the square and let it examine it. Then encourage it on a little until it puts one foot across the pole. Should it try to jump, stop it immediately. Only by progressing very slowly can you prevent it from doing so.

This exercise prepares you horse to tackle any obstacle on the ground with which you confront it and to trust your command. It is therefore an important part of obedience training. Practise this exercise whenever you have the opportunity. You can add variety to the exercise by experimenting with different arrangements of the ground poles, such as parallel poles (40-70 centimetres apart depending on the size of your horse), fan shaped poles or diamond-shaped arrangements. Take a look at the trail courses Western riders use for further inspiration.

The litter trail

The next obedience game has a really practical application. Any rider who has encountered problems with a horse on dustbin day should be working on this exercise. The aim is to walk alongside dustbins and bags lined up on the right. To the left is a rope with lots of bunting, flapping plastic tape or bags tied to it. Find a helper to shake the rope, while

you lead your horse through a passage about two metres wide.

Practise with as many differently coloured bins and arrangements of plastic bags, filled with straw or cardboard, as possible. Avoid sharp objects like tins, cans and hard plastic, as your horse could get injured should it be scared and jump into the bags.

Most horses are not frightened of the litter bags but are much more distracted by the shaking plastic tape. These movements cannot be judged well by the horse and the rustling noise provides an additional challenge.

Your horse should walk along the litter trail in as calm and relaxed a fashion as it did past the balloons. Again, allow plenty of time for your horse to become familiar with this challenge before expecting it to achieve that.

This pair walk along the litter trail in a calm fashion.

Movement creates fear

A horse's fear of moving objects is totally logical as it is based on their natural instincts. In the wild, predators rush towards them when preparing to attack. Still objects are therefore regarded as less dangerous.

Gradually increase the challenge

When you begin to work on the litter trail, start with just the bins. Let your horse have a good look at one first. You could try storing some feed in the bin, which will soon help any fear dissolve. Curiosity (and greed!) should win and the horse becomes more daring. Some horses even learn to open the lid in order to get to the food. Once he accepts a stationary bin, if they are wheelie bins, try pulling one along on one side, while leading the horse on the other.

The next step is to get your horse used to plastic rubbish bags. Once he is happy with those (and don't forget to try different colours), you could combine the two and walk your horse past the bins and bags.

Now the plastic tape. You can buy this type of tape in a DIY store; there are red-white and black-yellow tapes and sometimes other variations. Buy what you can get, but make sure that it will tear easily in case a scared horse runs or jumps into it. Some of the stronger tapes that are mainly used at building sites are not suited for this purpose.

A horse thus accustomed to bins, bags and plastic tape will walk through the litter passage without any problems. Of course, you should not hesitate yourself and must walk positively as, if you do not, you will signal your insecurity to your horse. Even a short wavering can lead to a problem.

Balls in the hedge

There are many circumstances in which something can suddenly run, roll or be blown out into the path of your horse as you are hacking. To accustom your horse to this occurrence, use balls rolled by a helper from a gap in an artificial hedge to teach your horse he has nothing to fear. You can use anything from a football to a larger exercise ball as shown in the photograph. The helper is advised to let the balls roll in front of the horse's legs and not underneath its belly, but it can of course happen that a ball ends up below the horse. Your horse should be prepared to cope with this situation calmly.

Even such large exercise balls are no cause for concern for this grey.

Expect the unexpected

Playing with balls can be part of your daily training regime. That way, your horse should stay calm when confronted by a stray football in the park or anything unexpected such as a rabbit or pheasant that may suddenly appear in front of him and could well scare you both. The ball exercise is very valuable for everyday life as quite often various objects can appear without warning that are not only a distraction for the horse but can initiate a flight reaction. What an advantage it is if your horse keeps calm then!

Practise stepping backwards so that your horse does this willingly and without hesitation.

Walking backwards

It is amazing how many horses resist stepping backwards in-hand. Even if they do this well when being ridden, it does not mean they are equally co-operative when led. Backing a horse demonstrates its obedience, and also the handler shows he or she has control over their horse.

Ask your horse to halt at a certain point and walk backwards between two markers on each side. Do not allow it to step over the markers and it should go backwards without hesitation.

Ideally you should not have to touch your horse but sometimes a slight pull of the rein is sufficient to back it. The subtler your aids are, the better.

Use fence poles to mark the area. The horse should walk backwards in a straight line in order to avoid touching them. More often than not, horses do not want to do this and swing to one side or the other. This can be for various reasons. Most horses bend more easily to one side than to another. If this natural imbalance is not improved through exercise, the horse will remain unable to step back in a straight line.

With appropriate aids you can compensate for your horse's natural twist. If, for example, your horse moves its hindquarters to the left, just pull the head slightly to the left. Although the horse then appears bent, it will step backwards in a straight line. Controlling the direction when backing a horse is always done from the position of the head. If you hold the head slightly to the left, the hindquarters will move in the opposite direction because the horse tries to straighten out. Depending on where you hold the head, your horse will step backwards straight or crooked.

Who really is the boss?

If a horse refuses to step backwards or only does it unwillingly, you have to find the reason for it.

First of all, your horse has to trust you, as it cannot see where it is going. Never walk your horse into an obstacle and do not use stepping back as a method of getting your horse into water, for example. Your horse will only lose its trust in you and will avoid going backwards in the future.

Sometimes, stepping back is a genuine battle. Some horses will challenge their owner to see who is really in control. Backing has a lot to do with surrender. Every low ranking horse has to give way to a higher ranking one and often by stepping backwards. Therefore, backing also means giving in, and strengthens the position of the human as higher ranking.

Stepping back as punishment?

Some trainers use backing as a method of punishment in order to gain control of their horse. Whilst it is possible to use backing for surrender it is, however, not recommended as afterwards your horse will not willingly back up any more and you could lose a valuable exercise.

Your horse should walk backwards actively and without force. You achieve that by giving subtle aids using the reins or lead rope. You can use your hand at first and put pressure on the horse's chest until it moves backwards. Increase the pressure if your horse is stub-

born and do not stop until it has given in. The animal will then learn that this uncomfortable pressure will only end if it steps in the desired direction. As soon as it has understood the principle, you will only need to give slight aids to make it move. Make sure that you release the pressure promptly as otherwise your horse might just resist your force.

Use the same voice command every time in order to back your horse. The more your training advances the less pressure you will need to use until the animal will react to your voice and a slight pull of the reins alone. If you then include body language as well, it will become even easier. Stand in front and slightly to one side of your horse and approach it in a confident way. If it does not give way be forceful! It is very important that you enforce the rules, as you have to remain the boss. But don't forget to reward him afterwards.

Do not ask for more than you can enforce in order not to end up being the loser. Be satisfied with one or two backward steps. Throughout the training, you can gradually increase the challenge and therefore the number of steps until your horse can be moved in any direction with subtle aids.

Practise moving your horse through various arrangements of poles in a forward, sideways and backward direction (as trail riders do). Your horse will then be sufficiently prepared to move backwards in between two markers in a straight line.

Umbrellas

Some horses appear to have no problem at all with umbrellas, whilst others are absolutely terrified. This game should help your horse to overcome his fears.

Once your horse trusts you to lead it past obstacles, secure in the knowledge that you will not put him in a position of danger, he will tend to treat umbrellas on the floor with curiosity rather than fear. However, the sudden opening of an umbrella is a different matter. Throughout any form of confidence training, you will

With good preparation, passing the umbrella challenge will not be a problem.

discover that motionless objects cause less fear than moving ones. As we have said before, this is based on natural instincts. This instinctive behavioural pattern can only be altered with lots of practice.

You can expect certain reactions depending on where the moving object is located. For example, if you open an umbrella below and to one side of a horse, it will be more frightened than if you do so at eye level. Previous experiences play a role here as well: if punishment has always come from behind (such as a schooling whip on the rump), a horse will be more scared of movements behind it.

When you first begin work on this game, rehearse the opening of the umbrella from all angles to discover what causes your horse the most problems. Will your horse remain calm when it cannot see the umbrella any more but only hears the noise? How will it react if it sees the moving umbrella from the corner of its eye?

There are other surprises with this obstacle. A sudden gust of wind could move the umbrellas on the floor. The helper might hold the umbrella very high up or very low. There are many stimuli influencing your horse. Therefore you should pay special attention to the training session with the umbrellas.

Introducing umbrellas correctly

Firstly, introduce your horse to an unopened umbrella and let it examine it thoroughly. Once it is happy with this, run the umbrella over its body, stopping before it becomes afraid. Make a big fuss of him. Repeat this process on another occasion, hopefully progressing a little further and continuing in this manner until your horse accepts the umbrella without problems.

The next stage is open umbrellas. Begin by slowly opening an umbrella as far as your horse will tolerate it without moving away. Increase the challenge until it accepts all possible positions, movements and contact. When you can move the umbrella in front of and behind the horse without it showing any reaction, you have reached your goal.

Now move on a step and try leading your horse along a two metre wide passage lined with umbrellas and a helper to open and close one, too. Make sure you walk your horse past the objects calmly and without hesitation.

Use several helpers with umbrellas who will position themselves at a distance, around the horse. Let them open their umbrellas at the same time or in waves and from all angles. Does your horse stay calm?

Don't scare your horse!

Remember when carrying out these exercises that you MUST NOT scare your horse. Watch carefully for any signs of fear or discomfort and always stop before things become scary.

The tarpaulin

Many horses are reluctant to step on something on the ground that they do not recognise. They interpret this as dangerous, which is why many horses refuse certain jumps.

Start your exercise slowly if your horse has difficulties with this object. Firstly, make sure that the obstacle is not dangerous. The tarpaulin should be lying flat on the ground without folds. If possible, cover the edges with plenty of sand to avoid the horse getting entangled in it with its feet and also ensure that it is weighted down and cannot blow away in the wind.

The larger the tarpaulin the less likely it is that the horse will try to walk past it or jump over it. Markers like fence poles or cones are helpful, too, as these provide an optical boundary and help fix the tarpaulin to the ground. Wooden fences, like the ones used

The tarpaulin does not present a problem for well-trained horses, even under the saddle.

to mark a dressage arena, are not suitable. If your horse gets scared and jumps into the fence it could get badly injured.

Choose a strong and resilient lorry tarpaulin or one from a DIY store. A length of 3.5 to 4 metres is recommended.

Rectangular sheets should be approached from the long side so that the horse does not think it can walk around it easily. You should now be well prepared for your training.

No studs please!

Make sure your horse does not have shoes with studs, no matter how strong the tarpaulin is. The studs can puncture the plastic and the horse might become entangled and drag it along, which may cause it to panic.

Keep practising

Horses have a tendency to lean against the handler when they become nervous. You have to be very careful that your horse does not step on your toes when trying to walk it across the tarpaulin. Teach your horse to keep a safe distance when being led. Make sure it walks across the sheet slowly. If it wants to run away, stop it, but do not make an animal that is frightened stand on the tarpaulin. That would be too much to cope with at this stage. Let it explore the sheet and only ask it to move on once it does not show much interest any more. By being patient, even a very nervous horse will soon dare to take that step.

It is important that you allow your horse to step back again should it still be too scared. Once it had one foot on the tarpaulin, it will do it again, if it hasn't had a bad experience. If, however, you stop your horse from moving backwards, the stress could be too much for it to cope with. Your horse will connect this stress with placing a foot on the sheet and it will be very reluctant to do it again.

With a lot of practice, your horse will gradually build the necessary trust and confidence required to master tarpaulins of all colours and in various locations.

Exploring the sheet

Allow your horse to lower its head towards the tarpaulin in order to express its interest and attention. Vigilant horses are better partners than those that do not care what they step on.

The rattling bag

Our penultimate challenge will prepare your horse for any scary noises from passing traffic or pedestrians. It consists of familiarizing it to the sounds made by a rattling bag full of something such as stones. This creates a lot of noise that can frighten the horse.

There are several ways in which this can be done. The horse can be led next to a person who drags a rattling bag behind them, or the bag can be dragged over an obstacle

Ears pointing towards the noise show the horse is paying attention but it trusts its leader and therefore stays calm and relaxed.

lying on the ground (see photograph). The rider can move the bag from one object, such as a barrel or bale of straw, onto another. Or, and most difficult of all, the bag can be pulled by the rider.

In order to prepare for this challenge, you need to accustom your horse to the bag first. As with all new objects, let your horse examine it initially. Then move the bag slightly to create a noise. Next, gently run the bag over the horse's body, but only for as long as he accepts it.

Once the horse tolerates the bag, tie it to a long rope and get a helper to drag it. The helper is advised to pull the bag slightly behind the horse.

There is danger

The fact that the rattling sound comes from behind causes many horses to become scared. The animal cannot see what is creating the noise and instinctively tries to flee to safety.

Practise pulling various objects – they can be branches, plastic sheets or tyres – so that your horse gets thoroughly used to this.

Halt on command

A horse is only a safe partner if it is obedient and can be controlled by its handler. The last test, standing still despite distractions, is particularly aimed at that. The horse has to stand motionless on a loose rein for about 30 seconds. In order to make this even harder, try playing noises on a tape after about 10 seconds or getting helpers to make as much noise as they can.

Most horses do not react to the noise but they will, nonetheless, not stand still. This unsettled behaviour is due to the fact that most horses have never learned to stand still when told. They are too impatient or are too interested in everything going on around them and do not concentrate on this task.

The example of Western riding

Western riders have integrated this so-called 'ground tying' into their regular training schedule. You can often see a single horse standing in the middle of an arena with loose reins while others canter around it. This horse will stand there motion-less waiting for its rider who, for example, just takes off his jacket or sets up a fence.

How do Western riders achieve this? First of all, you need a firm command for this task so that the horse knows what you want from

Standing still with an obedient and relaxed horse.

it. You can choose any word you like but you have to carry on using it. It is advised to select a word that has a calming sound, as it is easier for the horse to under-stand. A sharp "hey" is not suit-able, better are words like "haaaalt" or "hooooo".

When your horse is to stand still, stop it with the help of the reins and the verbal command. If it stands still, praise it. Then wait until the horse does not want to stand still any longer and begins to step forward or backward. Correct the step immediately and enforce the command with voice and reins. Repeat this a few times until your horse has managed to stand still for a while.

Do not overdo it at the beginning but be satisfied with 5 or 10 seconds and then walk the horse off – also using an appropriate command such as 'walk on'. Practise standing still every day and increase the time gradually. Ask for it when grooming and tacking up your horse. A horse should, of course, also stand still when the farrier and vet are around. As you can see, this exercise is very valuable for everyday situations and furthermore, a well-mannered horse will not step on your feet quite so often. Badly behaved horses, however, that do not want to stand still or simply ignore the people around them can be quite dangerous.

Incorporate confidence training into your routine on a regular basis.

Training at home

With confidence training, it is very important to practise continuously in order to get your horse used to the new ideas. Only then will progress become permanent. Therefore, a few elements of the training should be incorporated into your daily routine.

It is always an advantage to set yourself a realistic goal as it keeps you motivated. Such a goal could be, for example, for your horse to stand still while you tack him up, or that your horse learns to accept the rattling bag. You must be certain, however, that it is possible to achieve your goal for both you and your horse, because otherwise you will not succeed, which can be very demoralising. If you own a real problem horse that has had many bad experiences, you cannot expect the same results as you would from a horse that has had a good start in life, and may need professional help.

Make a plan of what you want to achieve with your horse but do not determine by when you should achieve these results. By setting a tight deadline, you will only increase the pressure on both of you.

Making the most of poles

You do not have to run through the complete training programme every day. If you have had a stressful day or the weather is particularly bad, or you and your horse simply do not feel on top form, a practice session can even be counter-productive. However, working with poles on a daily basis is usually beneficial. Poles offer so many variations that you and your horse certainly will not get bored. Using poles for relaxation, balance, circus tricks and obedience lessons adds interest, especially for horses that cannot be ridden.

The right circumstances
When practising with your horse, always stick to the basic principles. The human has to be the leader at all times. The horse must never question the higher rank of the handler. Disciplined behaviour is one of the basic elements that you need to ask for from your horse at all times. Only

then can you guarantee that your horse will be obedient – one of the prerequisites of successful work.

Only practise when your horse is well. If it is 'under the weather', for example shortly after a spell of colic, you should not ask it to work hard. This does not only apply to strenuous physical work like show jumping, but also to the intense concentration that working with poles requires.

It is also advisable that you only work with your horse when you feel well yourself. You should not bring your worries and stress to the stables. If you are short-tempered and impatient due to your own problems, you may compromise the whole training and will not make any progress.

Be prepared
Find a quiet and undisturbed environment. If your horse is distracted by playing children or barking dogs, your training will hardly be very successful.

Prepare your training session carefully. Make sure all required items are available before you fetch your horse from the stable or field. Is the schooling area suitable or is the sand school so flooded after heavy rain that you cannot walk in it? It is then better to postpone your session to another day. A pleasant atmosphere is as important for you as it is for your horse.

Working together with other people from your yard is a lot more fun and you can help each other or use a more experienced horse as a guide. Let the older horse walk across the dreaded tarpaulin and the nervous youngster will follow it. These methods can make many of the exercises a lot easier.

It is also very beneficial to have a helper when carrying out confidence building exercises or using poles. You can then concentrate completely on your horse while your helper opens the umbrella or adjusts the poles.

Make sure that you lead your horse from the opposite side to the fences so that it does it does not run into you if it gets frightened. A horse may ignore you when it is very scared and spooks. If you are in the way then that could be dangerous!

Another principle: only ever attempt to master an obstacle if you are sure that you and your horse can actually do it. Otherwise you may have to abandon your exercise, such as crossing the tarpaulin, unsuccessfully, which is a step backwards in the whole training regime. Increase the degree of difficulty gradually and always finish on a positive note. End the training with an easy task that your horse can fulfil comfortably and then praise it and turn it out in the field as a reward.

Practise with your horse in quiet surroundings and take plenty of time.

Training camp

For your own motivation, design your own individual training schedule. Create a varied programme but only practise with one or two challenges each day. Set a target that you want to achieve and make notes about each session.

Mark special achievements clearly, such as: "today my horse stepped on the tarpaulin for the first time!"

Take some video shots from time to time and analyse them, if possible with your trainer, and also pay attention to your own behaviour. Videos can be very revealing. Compare early footage with the latest and you will see what progress you and your horse have made already.

Take photos, as well, and add these to your training record. You will see how satisfactory it is to go back to them later and realise how good your horse has become in the meantime.

Do not be afraid to step back in your training programme if a certain exercise causes persistent problems. Maybe your horse is simply not ready for it yet. The decision to start right from the beginning again will be rewarded with a much better result at the end.

Are you relaxed yourself?

Horses are herd animals and they will always follow their companions. They trust a higher ranking animal and follow it faithfully. When they accept a human as a higher ranking herd member – or at least this is how it should be – a horse will follow a person and imitate their behaviour. Therefore if you are insecure or frightened, your horse will know that something is not right and it will become worried and scared as well.

The inner attitude with which you approach a challenge is therefore important. If you are nervous because you anticipate that your horse is going to be scared of an umbrella, the animal will notice your insecurity and indeed react to the umbrella with fear. If, however, you stay confident and calm, you can pass this on to your horse. It will not expect danger and will stay much calmer in what could be a difficult situation.

This is good practice for other situations such as a hack, on which you need to reassure your horse that there is nothing to worry about, or a competition, where you want to present your horse to the judges and other people in as good a light as possible. Even professionals feel a little bit tense or nervous sometimes and a horse will notice this and usually react in the same way.

There are two ways to overcome this phenomenon. The first is by acclimatisation - you can hack out and attend competitions until you and your horse have developed a certain routine and confidence. The second is to work on controlling your nerves and appearing calmer.

A horse can recognise its owner's mood immediately by body language and facial expressions.

Controlling yourself

It is important to control your nerves whenever you are out with your horse. However, at home too, you may not always be relaxed, but sometimes annoyed and stressed. You can pass on this anger that you take to the stables to your horse.

You may be impatient during the training or even aggressive. This aggression and impatience could be directed at your horse and you may punish it unnecessarily.

Horses can tell their owner's mood by body language and facial expression. It cannot tell, howev-

77

er, why their owner is so angry and it will become insecure and confused. If it is asked to fulfil a demanding task while the owner puts it under too much pressure, due to being in a bad mood, the whole situation can go wrong.

Normally, the effects are not dramatic, but it is bad enough if you are impatient and do not allow your horse the time it needs to get used to a new challenge. It is therefore important to not only exercise your horse but also think about yourself. You have to calm down first and switch off from the anger and the stress.

It is not easy, especially if you have had a hectic day at work or just had an argument with someone at the stables. Even if you put on a happy face and tell yourself that work is over, you could still be very stressed. It takes some time to truly calm down.

Special relaxation techniques can help you learn to calm down quicker. This makes working with the horse easier and more successful. In the end, training in a relaxed and calm environment is much more fun for both of you.

Autogenic training

One of the most popular relaxation techniques is autogenic training, AT for short. Developed by Prof. I.H. Schultz, he describes this method as "concentrated self-relaxation". With this technique,

you focus on a deep quietness, almost like a type of self-hypnosis.

It is necessary that you concentrate on certain events in your body. You focus on specific feelings (for example, warm and heavy feet) that stimulate the parasympathetic nervous system and actually produce the sensation in your body.

If you want to learn and to use autogenic training you require a lot of practice. The more often and regularly you exercise, the quicker you can produce the sensation in your body. In the end, your body reacts automatically to the triggers.

A trigger can be a phrase that you repeat in your head and it should be short and distinct. You will then notice a physical (relaxed) and realistic sensation while thinking about it. Overly tense efforts or very critical analysis of the method can act as a block.

Even if it is possible to teach yourself autogenic training, it is very difficult to do. It is far better to learn it at an evening class. Some medical clinics also offer courses.

Progressive muscle relaxation

In order to cope with stress in your everyday life, the method of progressive muscle relaxation (PMR) has been shown to be very effective. Many people find this method much more valuable as it is quite easy to apply.

You tense and hold various muscle groups one after the other and then very consciously relax them again. This way, you achieve a distinct physical state of relaxation that also influences your mind.

All moods, like feeling stressed, have a direct influence on your physical well-being. Your muscles become tense, often starting in the neck area, then the back and the whole body. By relaxing your muscles with this technique, you will also relax your mind.

This method can be learned fairly easily but special courses are helpful because you can learn how to address your individual problems better.

Other relaxation techniques

There are plenty of relaxation techniques. Most of them originate from foreign cultures that have been aware of the value of these methods. The methods used in eastern cultures are becoming especially popular.

Everyone has to determine which technique suits them best and then learn it thoroughly. Autogenic training and progressive muscle relaxation seem to be the methods of choice for most, but yoga and meditation are widely used too. Each method has its special advantages.

The benefit of yoga is that the exercises affect the whole body and have a general health value. It is highly recommended for horse riders.

Meditation can be seen as a progression from autogenic training. Your knowledge of your inner self will develop and you gain a better understanding of life cycles. You will learn to use your energy more efficiently and avoid wasting it on unnecessary actions.

Determine which relaxation technique suits you best and practise it every day for a few minutes. You will see that many everyday situations, as well as handling your horse, will become easier.

You will be more patient, will not get angry so quickly if an exercise does not work as planned and will be generally happier – together with your horse.

If you are relaxed, happy and calm, your horse will be less tense as well. You will then be a step closer to your dream of a cool and relaxed horse!

If you are cool, calm and relaxed, you will be closer to having the horse of your dreams.